Easy Steps to Buy a House & a Simplified Guide 2 Fix Your Credit

By Itzel Machado

Smashwords Edition

Copyright © 2012 Itzel Machado. All Rights Reserved.

No part of this book may be reproduced, stored in a retrieval system, or transmitted by any means without the written permission of the author.

Any people depicted in stock imagery provided by Thinkstock are models, and such images are being used for illustrative purposes only.

Certain stock imagery © Thinkstock. This book is printed on acid-free paper.

Because of the dynamic nature of the Internet, any web addresses or links contained in this book may have changed since publication and may no longer be valid. The views expressed in this work are solely those of the author and do not necessarily reflect the views of the publisher, and the publisher hereby disclaims any responsibility for them.

Preface

My experience, of 12 years, in the Real Estate industry drove an interest in trying to find ways to bring to light what one should expect when buying a house. By and large, there is scanty if any information on the topic. And for many years the most preeminent sources of such information, even for us in the industry, has always been famous one topic pamphlets titled "How to insure your home" not to mention others. Since there has been no significant movement towards availing such information much less any complete guide to buying a house, I took up a new challenge. I decided to write this book and make it affordable to everyone.

In the years that I have been working in Real Estate, I have been able to observe the progressive changes in the market; from the very traditional sales era where sellers had equity on their properties, so at closing they actually walked away with some leverage from the sale of their houses, to the declining prices of the market, and then, recently I was able to witness how prices hit rock bottom. However, I have never seen interest rates dip as low as the current ones we are having at the moment, perhaps this is the main reason why we, Realtors, are as busy as were a few years ago.

Prospective clients keep calling my office requesting for more and more information on the procedures as well as the logistics involved in the purchase of a house, even though every individual has diverse preferences and interests, the steps to buying a house are more or less similar. Indeed, enclosed you will find a short, summarized guide to help those who are interested in taking advantage of these rates that, I honestly believe, are here only for a short while. Time will pass before we experience the same situation.

Legal Disclaimer

The materials available on this book are for informational purposes only and not for the purpose of providing legal advice. You should contact your attorney to obtain advice with respect to any particular issue or problem.

The best way to approach a topic in writing is through a simple and easy to understand presentation, for this reason I chose the "Questionnaire" format to introduce this material. Keeping things simple and as short as possible is always the best, so here we go...

Are you ready to buy?

Knowledge and experience are the keys to successful real estate transactions.

One of the keys to making the home-buying process easier and more understandable is planning. In doing so, you'll be able to anticipate requests from lenders, lawyers and a host of other professionals. Furthermore, planning will help you discover valuable shortcuts in the home-buying process.

Do You Know What You Want?

Whether you are a first-time home buyer or entering the marketplace as a repeat buyer, you need to ask why you want to buy. Are you planning to move to a new community due to a lifestyle change or is buying an option and not a requirement? What would you like in terms of real estate that you do not now have? Do you have a purchasing timeframe?

Whatever your answers, the more you know about the real estate marketplace, the more likely you are to effectively define your goals. As an interesting exercise, it can be worthwhile to look at the questions above and to then discuss them in detail when meeting with local Realtors.

Do You Have The Money?

Homes and financing are closely intertwined. (Financing is the difference between the purchase price and the down payment, commonly referred to as debt or the mortgage.) The good news is that over the years new and innovative loan programs have evolved which require a 5 percent down payment or less.

In addition to a down payment, purchasers also need cash for closing costs (the final costs associated with closing the loan). Several newly emerging loan programs not only allow the purchase of a home with no money down, but also underwrite closing costs.

Not everyone, however, elects to purchase with little or no money down. Less money down means higher monthly mortgage payments, so most home buyers choose to buy with some cash up front.

As to closing costs, in markets where buyers have leverage, it may be possible to negotiate an offer for a home that requires the owner to pay some or all of your settlement expenses. Speak with local Realtors for details.

Is Your Financial House in Order?

Those great loans with little or nothing down are not available to everyone: You need good credit. For at least one year prior to purchasing a home, you should assure that every credit card bill, rent check, car payment and other debt is paid in full and on time.

Get a Realtor

More than 2 million people in the United States have earned real estate licenses. However, real estate is a tough business with a steep dropout rate, and the result is that only a small percentage of those with licenses actively help buyers and sellers.

The National Association of Realtors (NAR) includes 1 million brokers and salespeople, individuals bound together with a strong Code of Ethics, extensive training opportunities and a wealth of community information. NAR members are routinely active in PTAs, local government committees and a variety of neighborhood organizations. Being actively involved in community affairs provides Realtors with a better understanding of the area in which they are selling.

Why do I need a Realtor?

Buying and selling real estate is a complex matter. At first it might seem that by checking local picture books or online sites you could quickly find the right home at the right price.

But a basic rule in real estate is that all properties are unique. No two properties -- even two identical models on the same street -- are precisely and exactly alike. Homes differ and so do contract terms, financing options, inspection requirements and closing costs. Also, no two transactions are alike.

In this maze of forms, financing, inspections, marketing, pricing and negotiating, it makes sense to work with professionals who know the community and much more. Those professionals are the local Realtors who serve your area.

How do you choose?

In every community you're likely to find a number of realty brokerages. Because there is heated competition, local Realtors must fight hard to succeed in your community.

The best place to find a local Realtor is from REALTOR.com's extensive listing of community professionals and properties. Other sources include open houses, local advertising, Web sites, referrals from other Realtors, recommendations from neighbors and suggestions from lenders, attorneys, financial planners and CPAs. The experiences and recommendations of past clients can be invaluable.

In many cases buyers will interview several real estate agents before selecting one professional with whom to work. These interviews represent a good opportunity to consider such issues as training, experience, representation and professional certifications.

What should you expect when you work with a Realtor?

Once you select a Realtor you will want to establish a proper business relationship. You likely know that some Realtors represent sellers while others represent buyers. Each Realtor will explain the options available describe how he or she typically works with individuals and provide you with complete agency disclosures (the ins and outs of your relationship with the agent) as required in your state.

Once hired for the job, the Realtor will provide you with information detailing current market conditions, financing options and negotiating issues that might apply to a given situation. Remember: Because market conditions can change and the strategies that apply in one negotiation may be inappropriate in another, this information should not be set in stone. During your time in the marketplace real estate agents will keep you updated and alert you to each step in the transaction process.

Get Loan Pre approval

Few people can buy a home for cash. According to the National Association of REALTORS® (NAR), nearly nine out of 10 buyers finance their purchase, which means that virtually all buyers -especially first-time purchasers- required a loan.

The real issue with real estate financing is not getting a loan (virtually anyone willing to pay lofty interest rates can find a mortgage). Instead, the idea is to get the loan that's right for you -- the mortgage with the lowest cost and best terms.

Realtors routinely suggest that consumers start the mortgage process well before bidding on a home. Many lenders (the sources of money) and programs, for example, are available right here in the finance section of Realtor.com as well as through recommendations from local realtors. By meeting with lenders -- either online or face to face -- and looking at loan options, you will find which programs best meet your needs and how much you can afford.

Real estate agents also recommend pre approvals for another reason: Purchase forms often require buyers to apply for financing within a given time period, in many cases, seven to 10 days. By meeting with loan officers in advance and identifying mortgage programs, it won't be necessary to quickly find a lender, check credit, and rush into a financing decision that may not be the best option.

What is it?

"Pre-approval" means you have met with a loan officer, your credit files have been reviewed and the loan officer believes you can readily qualify for a given loan amount with one or more specific mortgage programs. Based on this information, the lender will provide a pre-approval letter, which shows your borrowing power. You can visit as many lenders as you like and get several pre-approvals, but keep in mind that each one carries with it a new credit check, which will show up on future credit reports.

Although not a final loan commitment, the pre-approval letter can be shown to listing brokers when bidding on a home. It demonstrates your financial strength and shows that you have the ability to go through with a purchase. This information is important to owners since they do not want to accept an offer that is likely to fail because financing cannot be obtained.

How do you get pre-approval?

Real estate financing is available from numerous sources, including lenders here in the finance section of Realtor.com, mortgage companies that have worked with local realtors and in some cases, individual Realtors themselves. Based on his or her experience, the Realtor may suggest one or more lenders with a history of offering competitive programs and delivering promised rates and terms.

The loan officer will carefully review your financial situation, including your credit report and other information. The lender will then suggest programs which most-closely meet your needs. For instance, a first-time buyer may qualify for state-backed mortgage programs with little money down and low interest rates, while a repeat purchaser (someone who has bought a home before) with more equity (money invested in the home) might want to get a 15-year loan and the lower overall interest costs it represents. Typically, first-time buyers opt for the traditional 30-year loan, with either a floating interest rate or a fixed rate of interest over the life of the loan.

Look at Homes

Millions of new and existing homes are sold each year. There's no shortage of housing options, but with so many choices the challenge becomes finding the property which best meets your needs.

The housing market is complicated because the stock of homes for sale is always in flux. If it were possible to have a complete list of every home for sale at this very moment in a given community, such a list would become obsolete within seconds as new homes become available and properties now for sale are put under contract.

In effect, buyers are looking at a moving target in a marketplace that is never static. Because of this, it is important to know as much as possible about the choices in preferred markets, and the way to do that is by working closely with a local Realtor who has a good lay of the land.

What are you looking for?

A home is more than just a collection of bedrooms and bathrooms. Several properties each with four bedrooms, three baths, and the same price may well represent radically different designs, commuting distances, lot sizes, tax costs, interior dimensions, and exterior finishes.

Each of us is different and so it's important to list the features and benefits you want in a home. Consider such things as pricing, location, size, amenities (extras such as a pool or extra-large kitchen) and design (one floor or two, colonial or modern, etc.).

Next, it's important to consider your priorities. If you can't get a home at your price with all the features you want, then what features are most important? For instance, would you trade fewer bedrooms for a larger kitchen? A longer commute for a bigger lot and lower cost?

Lastly, consider your needs in several years. If you'll need a larger home, maybe now is the time to buy a bigger house rather than moving or expanding in the future. If you expect your income to increase, perhaps you should consider a more expensive home financed with a loan program where monthly payments increase in the future.

Where should you look?

All neighborhoods and communities have a special nature that gives them identity and value. One community may be well known for historic homes while another offers both suburban living as well as easy access to downtown office areas.

How do you find a house?

Some buyers like to search local home finding websites called MLS (Multiple Listing Service). Looking at listings on the basis of location or price; others prefer to have local real estate agents suggest properties; and many buyers prefer both approaches.

Regardless of your choice, it's important to target your search. By using basic measures such as general location and affordability, you can refine your search and focus on homes that offer the most desirable features.

As a guide, you should maintain a file with information on each of the homes you like. You can print out listing pages from these local MLS systems and then make notes for each one what you like.

Choose a Home

There's no doubt that choosing a home is a big decision and you want to do it right.

As a buyer, here's what actually happens. A home has been placed on the market for which the seller has established an asking price as well as other terms. In effect, this is an offer. At this point, you have three choices: accept the seller's offer and create a contract; reject it and not make an offer; or suggest different terms and make a counter-offer. If you choose this last option, the seller may accept, reject or make a counter-offer.

No aspect of the home buying process is more complex, personal or variable than bargaining between buyers and sellers. This is the point where the value of an experienced Realtor is clearly evident because he or she knows the community, has seen numerous homes for sale, knows local values and has spent years negotiating realty transactions.

Is it THE house?

A house is shelter, but a home is far more. It's where you live, relax, entertain friends, raise families, and work. A home is where you spend much of your life, and so choosing a house is an enormous decision.

How do you know if a house is THE one? Probably the best approach is to look at as many homes as possible, something made easy by Realtor.com, where you can quickly and easily view huge numbers of homes, check prices, take video tours and view extensive neighborhood information. Once your choices have been narrowed, you can then contact a local Realtor to find specific information and options.

Can you really afford it?

Remember Step 2 - the pre-approval process? Getting pre-approved means you have a very good idea of how much you can borrow, what loan programs will most likely work best in your situation and how much home you can afford.

How reliable is a pre-approval? While pre-approval is not a loan commitment, it's still necessary for lenders to check such items as appraisals and the latest credit reports. Despite fluctuating interest rates, pre-approval nonetheless provides a reasoned, careful analysis of what you can afford. After all, loan officers are routinely paid only when loans are originated. It doesn't make much sense for loan officers to suggest high loan limits that later can't be delivered.

Get Funding

Often the cost of real estate financing is routinely greater than the original purchase price of a home (after including interest and closing costs). Because financing is so important, buyers should have as much information as possible regarding mortgage options and costs.

Realtor.com® provides consumers with extensive mortgage information as well as a variety of loan calculators. Local Realtors can provide mortgage information, discuss financing options and recommend loan sources. In addition, some real estate agents also originate loans.

What kind of loan?

There are thousands of loans available out there from a variety of lenders, but in general, the mortgage you choose will likely be determined by at least several key factors:

• How much down? Loans with 5 percent down or less are available -- in fact, loans from major lenders with no money down have appeared in recent years.

• If you place less than 20 percent down, lenders will want the mortgage guaranteed by an outside third party such as the Veterans Administration (VA), the Federal Housing Administration (FHA) or a private mortgage insurer (PMI, or private mortgage insurance, is required by lender to protect against any mortgage defaults). Millions of VA, FHA and PMI loans are generated each year.

• How's your credit? The best rates and terms are only available to those with solid credit. To get the best loans, make a point of paying credit cards, installment payments, rent and mortgage bills in full and on time.

• Are you a first-time buyer? It might seem that "first-time buyer" means someone who has never owned property before, but under most state programs, the term refers to those who have not owned property within the past three years. State-backed first-timer programs often feature smaller down payments and below-market interest rates. For details, speak with your local Realtor.

How do you get a loan?

To obtain a loan you must complete a written loan application and provide supporting documentation. Specific documents include recent pay stubs, rental checks and tax returns for the past two or three years if you are self-employed. During the prequalification procedure, the loan officer will describe the type of paperwork required.

Where do you get a loan?

Mortgage financing can be obtained from mortgage bankers, mortgage brokers, savings and loan associations, mutual savings banks, commercial banks, credit unions, and insurance companies. A growing number of Realtors can also arrange financing

Make an Offer

Realtors groups, working with legal counsel, have developed forms that are appropriate for realty transactions in specific communities. Such documents include numerous sale conditions and their wording should be carefully reviewed to assure that they reflect the terms you want to offer. Realtors can explain the general contracting process in your community as well as his or her role.

While much attention is spent on offering prices, a proposal to buy includes both the price and terms. In some cases, terms can represent thousands of dollars in additional value for buyers -- or additional costs. Terms are extremely important and should be carefully reviewed.

How much?

You sometimes hear that the amount of your offer should be x percent below the seller's asking price or y percent less than you're really willing to pay. In practice, the offer depends on the basic laws of supply and demand: If many buyers are competing for homes, then sellers will likely get full-price offers and sometimes even more. If demand is weak, then offers below the asking price may be in order.

How do you make an offer?

The process of making offers varies around the country. In a typical situation, you will complete an offer that the Realtor will present to the owner and the owner's representative. The owner, in turn, may accept the offer, reject it or make a counter-offer.

Because counter-offers are common (any change in an offer can be considered a "counter-offer"), it's important for buyers to remain in close contact with Realtor during the negotiation process so that any proposed changes can be quickly reviewed.

How many inspections?

A number of inspections are common in residential realty transactions. They include checks for termites, surveys to determine boundaries, appraisals to determine value for lenders, title reviews and structural inspections.

Structural inspections are particularly important. During these examinations, an inspector comes to the property to determine if there are material physical defects and whether expensive repairs and replacements are likely to be required in the next few years. Such inspections for a single-family home often require two or three hours, and buyers should attend. This is an opportunity to examine the property's mechanics and structure, ask questions and learn far more about the property than is possible with an informal walk-through.

Get Insurance

No one would drive a car without insurance, so it figures that no homeowner should be without insurance.

The essential idea behind various forms of real estate insurance is to protect owners in the event of catastrophe. If something goes wrong, insurance can be the bargain of a lifetime.

What kind and how much?

There are various forms of insurance associated with home ownership, including these major types:

Title insurance: Purchased with a one-time fee at closing, title insurance protects owners in the event that title to the property is found to be invalid. Coverage includes "lenders" policies, which protect buyers up to the mortgage value of the property, and "owners" coverage, which protects owners up to the purchase price. In other words, "owners" coverage protects both the mortgage amount and the value of the down payment.

Homeowners' insurance: Homeowner's insurance provides fire, theft and liability coverage. Homeowners' policies are required by lenders and often cover a surprising number of items, including in some cases such property as wedding rings, furniture and home office equipment.

Flood insurance: Generally required in high-risk flood-prone areas, this insurance is issued by the federal government and provides as much as $250,000 in coverage for a single-family home plus $100,000 for contents. Local Realtors can explain which locations require such coverage.

Home warranties: With new homes, buyers want assurance that if something goes wrong after completion the builder will be there to make repairs. But what if the builder refuses to do the work or goes out of business?

Home warranties bought from third parties by home builders are generally designed to provide several forms of protection: workmanship for the first year, mechanical problems such as plumbing and wiring for the first two years, and structural defects for up to 10 years.

Home warranties for existing homes are typically one-year service agreements purchased by sellers. In the event of a covered defect or breakdown, the warranty firm will step in and make the repair or cover its cost.

Insurance policies and warranties have limitations and individual programs have different levels of coverage, deductibles and costs. For details, speak with realtors, insurance brokers and home builders.

How do you get insurance?

The time to obtain insurance and warranty coverage right before closing, so speak with a Real estate agent or insurance broker prior to closing. Be sure to ask about limitations, costs, deductibles and "endorsements" (additional forms of coverage that may be available).

Closing

The closing process, which in different parts of the country is also known as "settlement" or "escrow," is increasingly computerized and automated. In many cases, buyers and sellers don't need to attend a specific event; signed paperwork can be sent to the closing agent via overnight delivery.

In practice, closings bring together a variety of parties who are part of the "transaction" process. For example, while the history of property ownership has been checked, it's possible that the records contain errors, unrecorded claims or flaws in the review itself, thus title insurance is necessary. At closing, transfer taxes must be paid and other claims must also be settled (including closing costs, legal fees and adjustments). In most transactions, the closing agent also completes the paperwork needed to record the loan.

What to expect

Settlement is a brief process where all of the necessary paperwork needed to complete the transaction is signed. Closing is typically held in an office setting, sometimes with both buyer and seller at the same table, sometimes with each party completing their papers separately.

Whatever the case, the result is that title to the property is transferred from seller to buyer. The buyer receives the keys and the seller receives payment for the home. From the amount credited to the seller, the closing agent subtracts money to pay off the existing mortgage and other transaction costs. Deeds, loan papers, and other documents are prepared, signed and filed with local property record offices.

What you need to do

One of the best parts of settlement is that buyers and sellers need to do very little.

Before closing, buyers typically have a final opportunity to walk through the property to assure that its condition has not materially changed since the sale agreement was signed. At closing itself, all papers have been prepared by closing agents, title companies, lenders and lawyers. This paperwork reflects the sale agreement and allows all parties to the transaction to verify their interests. For instance, buyers get the title to the property, lenders have their loans recorded in the public records and state governments collect their transfer taxes.

What's Next?

You've done it. You've looked at properties, made an offer, obtained financing and gone to closing. The home is yours. Is there any more to the home buying process?

Whether you're a first-time buyer or a repeat buyer, there are several more steps you'll want to take.

Those papers you received at settlement are extremely valuable, so hold on to them! In the short-term they can help establish tax deductions for the year in which the property was purchased. In the future, such papers will be important for tax purposes when the property is sold, and in some cases, for calculating estate taxes.

Also at closing, determine the status of the utilities required by the home, items such as water, sewage, gas, electric and oil service. You want utility bills to be paid in full by owners as of closing and you also want services transferred to your name for billing. Usually such transfers can be done without turning off utilities. Realtors can provide contact numbers and related information.

About two weeks after closing, contact your local property records office and confirm that your deed has been officially recorded. Such records are public notices that show your interest in the property.

Moving in

It is generally understood that sellers will leave homes "broom clean" when moving out. This expression does not mean "vacuumed" or "spotless." Broom clean makes sense because it means the house is ready to be painted and cleaned.

Your home, your money

For most owners a home is the largest single asset they hold, so it makes sense to protect that asset.

Many owners make a photo or video record of the home and their possessions for insurance purposes and then keep the records in a safety deposit box. Your insurance provider can recommend what to photograph and how to secure it.

You want to maintain fire, theft and liability insurance. As the value of your property increases such coverage should also rise. Again, speak with your insurance professional for details.

Lastly, enjoy your home. Owning real estate involves contracts, loans, and taxes, but ultimately what's most important is that home ownership should be a wonderful experience. Enjoy!

Take Control of Your Credit Today

Many people have removed negatives items from their reports using the methods on this page. Indeed, everything a credit repair company can do for you, you can do for yourself at a fraction of the cost.

Sometimes people feel overwhelmed with the credit repair process and want to ask a live person a question if they get stumped; you still have this option available if you decide to work on your own credit. The three mayor credit bureaus have a customer service line available to anybody with a question.

The information provided on this page is intended to help you fix errors on your credit report and clean up those "questionable" items. While no one can legally remove ACCURATE negative information from a credit report, the law does allow you to request an investigation of information in your file that you dispute as inaccurate or incomplete

Remember: "There is no charge for requesting an investigation". The whole key to the credit repair procedure is that if the credit bureaus cannot verify information on your credit report, they must remove it. For instance, if a credit bureau cannot contact a collection agency which is reporting a collection on your report, they cannot verify the information, and the credit bureau must delete the entry

Basic Steps to Repairs Your Credit

The basic strategy to repairing your credit is as follows:

1. Get and Review your credit as soon as possible.

2. Analyze your report.

3. Make a list of all items you consider to be questionable or negative. Clearly identify each item in your report you are disputing and explain why you are disputing this information.

4. Write a dispute letter to the credit bureaus.

5. Mail the letter to the credit bureaus. Make sure you send it registered or certified mail.

6. Document your efforts. Record when you sent your letters, and the results.

7. Wait for the bureaus to investigate your claims.

8. Analyze the results

9. Repeat

10. Specialized techniques .Was the item deleted or changed to your satisfaction? You may continue steps 1, 2 and 3 above until you feel the dispute is settled satisfactorily. Remember, there is no charge for a reinvestigation. If you don't get the results you want, dispute the listing again.

11. Should I dispute personal information?

12. What if a removed negative item and comes back on my credit report?

13. Feelings overwhelmed by this process or you don't have the time to do it? At first it seems easy enough but

you must have patience, because the credit bureaus are not always very cooperative. They make their money by providing credit reports to lenders not by fixing bad information in their databases.

ANSWERS:

1. Get Your Credit Report

If you want to obtain free copies of your report, you must know that when you get a free report, you are not going to see your credit score, which is a crucial tool in getting your credit in shape, for this reason I recommend you to invest few dollar on getting a complete credit report.

There are plenty of websites from which you'll be able to buy it from, just make sure it says "Three bureaus credit report", which are: Experian, Transunion and Equifax.

The following link will allows you to request a free credit report annually:

http://www.ftc.gov/bcp/edu/microsites/freereports/index.shtml

2. Analyze Your Credit Report

Once paying for your credit reports & scores online, you can download your report and saved it to your computer. After reviewing your credit report, you can print it out and then highlighted everything you see as a negative listing. Usually most of the negatives items my clients find are medical collections, and these are easy to spot. However, occasionally, they noticed that one of the bureaus was reporting a late payment on one of their credit cards, and they knew it was paid it on time, so this was a good reason for them to start a dispute right the way with the bureaus. Remember that you will need proof of on time payment to be attached to the dispute letter you will send to them.

The following link will help you analyze your credit report and will give you a pretty good idea where you credit report is at.

http://www.gotcredit.com/good-number-for-credit-score

3. Rank Questionable/Negative Items

Now that you have your list of negative items, you should rank each item according to the amount of damage it is doing to your overall credit picture. Rank the most damaging first, followed by the next most damaging, followed by those items which are neutral. Do this for each credit report, and remember, they may not all have the same information on them. They may even have duplicate information on them. If this is the case, you will need to write to each credit agency individually for each duplicate item.

The following items here are listed in order of "most damaging" to "least damaging" to your credit:

• Bankruptcy

- Foreclosure
- Repossession
- Loan Default
- Court Judgments
- Collections
- Past due payments
- Late Payments
- Credit Rejections
- Credit Inquiries

Also, if your creditor has NOT notified you of negative information they have recently placed on your credit report, they are currently in violation of the Fair Credit Reporting Act. You can use this to pressure the original creditor to remove the listing by reminding them they are in violation of the FCRA by not notifying you.

4. Requesting Corrections and Disputing Your Credit

What should you challenge?

Everything - and you should always shoot for a complete deletion. In your initial challenge, don't dispute the information within a collection listing, charge-off, court record, repossession, foreclosure, or settled account. Save disputing the information within the listing for the NEXT ROUND OF DISPUTES Start off the reason for your dispute on a negative listing whenever possible as "not mine". Here is a list of the most common dispute reasons:

1. Not mine or not my account.
2. I didn't pay late that month.
3. Wrong amount.
4. Wrong account number.
5. Wrong original creditor.
6. Wrong charge-off date.
7. Wrong date of last activity.
8. Wrong balance.
9. Wrong credit limit.
10. Wrong status - there are about 20 of these.
11. Wrong high credit - the highest amount you used.

What items are the toughest to get off your report?

You will have the toughest time getting bankruptcies, judgments, child support and foreclosures off of your credit report as these things are not so easy for the credit bureaus to verify electronically. In the case of a bankruptcy, you most likely will have a few trade lines saying "included in bankruptcy". If you want to challenge your bankruptcy, you need to clear off all credit lines mentioning a BK FIRST.

5. Mail All Letters Registered or Certified

This is important, as you must be able document when the letters were sent and received. This gives you some leverage with the CRAs if they don't respond in the time frame required by law. Tip: DON'T USE THE ONLINE DISPUTING SERVICE PROVIDED BY THE CREDIT BUREAUS. You need to be documenting everything, and you want to make sure that you have a complete record of your disputes. (This one is "a must follow").

6. Document Your Credit Repair Efforts

As soon as you have ordered your credit reports and photocopied your order letters and checks, you must create a precise organizational system to track your correspondences with the credit bureaus and your creditors. Why is this necessary? Unfortunately, credit items you have worked so hard to remove mysteriously reappear. If this happens, it is usually easy to have the items deleted permanently if you show your complete records on the first removal. Why take a chance?

As you proceed through these steps, keep copies and records of all correspondence you send and receive. Copies of all correspondence are a must, as well as notes on all telephone conversations! Also, if you should encounter any special difficulty and would like help in repairing your credit, you will need these records to proceed.

Every time you have a telephone conversation with a creditor, you must document the conversation by recording the name of the person to whom you spoke, his or her position, the date and time of the conversation, what was said in the conversation, and what was agreed upon.

7. Wait for the Credit Bureau to Investigate

Once the credit reporting agency has received your dispute letter, they are obligated to investigate. This obligation is not contingent upon you having been denied credit. According to the Fair Credit Report Act, the credit bureaus must take the following steps:

• The credit reporting agencies must resolve consumers' disputes within 30 days limit, unless you have used the services of annualcreditreport.com, then the bureaus can take up to 45 days.

• In response to consumers' complaints that documentation in support of their disputes was disregarded, the credit bureaus have to consider and transmit to the furnisher all relevant evidence submitted by the consumer the first time.

• Consumers will receive written notice of the results of the investigation within five days of its completion, including a copy of the amended credit file if it changed based on the dispute.

• Once information is deleted from a credit file, the credit bureaus cannot reinsert it unless the entity supplying the information certifies that the item is complete and accurate and the credit bureau notifies the consumer within five days.

The Federal Trade Commission says that inaccurate credit reports are the number-one source of consumer complaints, and it is quite common for problems to take six or more months to be resolved. All of the big-three agencies are working on making sure that all disputes are handled within 30 days.

If the new investigation reveals an error, you may ask that a corrected version of the report be sent to anyone who received your report within the last six months. Job applicants can have corrected reports sent to anyone who received a report for employment purposes during the past two years. However, this is unlikely to repair any damage done when your credit report was first pulled, so don't waste your time or energy on this approach.

8. Analyze the Results

You did save the original credit report your ordered, didn't you? And each item you challenged? Good, you will need them to evaluate how well you did. It's all part of Step 5 above, documenting your efforts.

When you get your "repaired" credit report back from the credit bureaus, they will summarize what changed on your credit report due to your challenges. You can compare this report to your notes or to the previous credit report.

The results of each item will have been resolved in one of the following ways:

1. If the listing is not mentioned in the results list, you must have forgotten to include it, or your request was not sufficiently clear. You will need to dispute that item again in

your next dispute letter. The bureaus are legally obligated to respond in writing within 30 days, so if they don't, it is highly unlike they are ignoring you.

2. The disputed item was investigated but verified. If the item was not removed, most likely, the credit bureaus just gave you a cryptic reason like "item verified. The law states the bureaus can accept any proof you would like to submit and they will pass this documentation on to your creditor for consideration. So, be sure to send any and all documentation, if you didn't do it the first time. I would also hit them up with the Method of Verification technique, which is going to force them to expose the fact that they are using eOscar, an online source ONLY (which shouldn't be the only one they contacted). You could also try disputing the listing again at a future time. Who knows, you may get lucky, and a different employee of the creditor may not be able to verify the item. If the account does come back as "verified", I recommend you try Disputing Listing with Original Creditor immediately.

3. The disputed listing was investigated as to the correctness of the information within the listing (such as late pay notations) and the listing was found to be inaccurate or unverifiable. Remember, if the creditor doesn't respond to the bureau at all, this is the same as the listing being unverifiable. In this case, the negative listing will now show up as a positive listing, or it will be deleted from your report all together. This is the best possible outcome.

9. Repeat Your Credit Bureau Dispute

Keep disputing negative listings with the credit bureaus. If you hit on the right dispute, the listing could get completely removed from your report. For instance, if you dispute the date the account was opened, and the credit bureaus cannot verify this information they delete the entire listing. You will need to change the reason for the investigation so the credit bureaus will have something new to investigate. The order of the reasons should be:

1. Not mine or not my account.

2. I didn't pay late that month.

3. Wrong amount.

4. Wrong account number.

5. Wrong original creditor.

6. Wrong charge-off date.

7. Wrong date of last activity.

8. Wrong balance.

9. Wrong credit limit.

10. Wrong status - there are about 20 of these.

11. Wrong high credit - the highest amount you used.

For example, the first time you challenge a listing, you might say the account is "not mine." The second time through, you could say "never late."

Tips for resubmitting your credit dispute:

• Be Persistent: Become more insistent, but not more threatening, with the each dispute.

• Make sure your letters are clear and to the point.

• Be Creative: Create and utilize other techniques that may help further the idea the dispute letter is from a truly wronged and disadvantage consumer. They are only interested in investigating disputes which are truly erroneous and damaging.

• Do not bombard the Credit Bureaus with disputes (about the same listings). Sending one dispute right after another is wasteful and counterproductive even if you do use a different reason in your dispute.

• Be Assertive: If you feel the credit bureaus are ignoring your disputes handling them incorrectly, you can mention that you are thinking of hiring an attorney. For instance, if your request for an investigation goes longer than 30 days the credit bureau is in violation of the law.

10. Specialized Techniques

Depending on the type of listing, you may also want to try these specialized techniques:

• **Collections** - This is actually an easy type of listing to deal with

• **Charge-Offs** - Try disputing the information within the listing, like the date the account was opened, the high balance, the amount owed, etc. If any of the information is incorrect, you have a good chance of getting the whole thing deleted off of your report.

• **Judgments** - If you were never served for a judgment, you may have a chance of getting it vacated (voided), or there may be other technicalities that you can use. Google it: "Vacating Judgments" on how to do this.

• **Dispute directly with the Original Creditor** - If well-spread out disputes with the credit bureaus does not work, you can always contact the Creditors directly and dispute your item with them

11. Should I Dispute Personal Information?

Absolutely! Making sure your name and address are correct is critical and prevents getting someone else's information on your report. Getting someone else's information on your report is called merging. The chances of having your credit report merged with another person's is higher than the bureaus will admit. It's happened to me. The reason for this mix up? A credit bureaus matched your wrong information (like a misspelled name or address) with someone else's and their items suddenly appear on your report.

The other reason you should clean up your personal information as it can gain you an advantage in credit repair. For example, sometimes a disputed account will have an address (like your old address) that does not appear on your report any longer. This can be reason enough for the bureau to delete the disputed account.

Some Helpful Tips:

• You should make sure only your **current address** is shown on your report. I had someone else's information appear on my report because their current address matched my former address.

• Only your full legal name should be on your report. This is especially important if your name is a common one.

• Check to make sure your social security number is correct. Incorrect SSNs are the number one reason reports get merged.

• Your current employer only should appear on your report, not your full employment history.

• When disputing this information, use words like "I've never lived here before", "This is not my address", "I've never worked here", or "My Social Security is not correct".

12. What if a Removed Negative Item Comes Back on my Credit Report?

Ok, you've removed a negative listing and are breathing a deep sigh of relief. Then you get a letter in the mail from a credit bureau telling you the item has been added back on. What happened?

Re-verified Listings

Unfortunately, this is actually becoming more common. Since the new credit laws require that the bureaus investigate and resolve your disputes within 30 days, they will sometimes remove the negative information temporarily until they get the information verified as true. Then they will put back any information verified to be true and notify you of this. By law, they can do this, but they have to notify you in writing.

If they DO NOT notify you in writing, it is an instant violation of the FCRA with a $1,000 fine PAYABLE TO YOU. Many people have had great success earning some easy cash by suing the credit bureaus for reinserted listings. Not only do you earn thousands, but the listing is removed from your report as well!

13. What if I Get Stuck?

If you have a question? Remember, you can always contact the credit bureaus directly.

Credit Reporting Agencies:

• **Equifax** 1-800-685-1111 - you can get a free report if you have been denied credit in the last 60 days. Make sure that you order only the credit report. Mail it within 48 hours.

• **TransUnion** 1-800-916-8800 - receive within 6 to 8 business days.

• **Experian** 1-888-397-3742 - receive within 8 to 10 business days.

Caution: If your phone request gets lost, you'll have to write to them anyway. If your letter is after 30 days of being denied credit, employment, or insurance, you might have to pay for the report.

It would be a good idea to mention in your letter the date that you requested the report by phone. Your written request should contain proof of your identity and current address, such as your driver's license and a copy of a utility bill.

Addresses for Credit Bureaus

Experian

P.O. Box 9556

Allen, TX 75013

Equifax

P.O. Box 740241

Atlanta, GA 30374-0241

TransUnion

Trans Union Consumer Relations

P.O. Box 2000

Chester, PA 19022-2000

When mailing your request, make sure you send all of the information previously mentioned.

General Contact Numbers

Experian

Office in TX: 1-888-397-3742

Business: 1-888-211-0728

Equifax

Business Line (also has option for Personal): 1-888-202-4025

Office in GA: 1-800-685-1111

Dispute Fax #: 1-888-826-0573

Business: 1-802-304-0364

General: 1-800-797-6801

TransUnion

Office in PA: 1-800-888-4213

1-888-259-6845

1-800-916-8800 (consumer relations)

Made in the USA
Lexington, KY
23 October 2016